THE WORLD'S GREAT CLASSIC

The Baroque Era

53 Selections from Keyboard Literature, Concertos, Chamber Works, Oratorios & Operas for Piano Solo

EDITED BY BLAKE NEELY AND RICHARD WALTERS

Cover Painting: Jan van der Heyden, *View of the Boterbrug with the Tower of the Stadhuis, Delft,* c. 1656

ISBN 0-634-04806-6

7777 W. BLUEMOUND RD. P.O. BOX 13819 MILWAUKEE, WI 53213

Visit Hal Leonard Online at
www.halleonard.com

CONTENTS

Keyboard Pieces

Transcriptions for Piano

The Windmill
(Le moulin à vent)

François Dagincourt
1684–1758

*The pincé, played

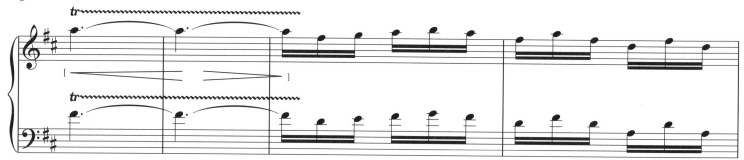

Canzonetta

Dietrich Buxtehude
1637–1707

Aria
from GOLDBERG VARIATIONS

Johann Sebastian Bach
1685–1750
BWV 988

[Lento con moto]

French Suite No. 2 in C Minor

Johann Sebastian Bach
1685-1750
BWV 813

Allemande
[Allegro moderato]

Courante
[Vivace]

Sarabande
[Andantino]

Air
[Andante]

1.

Menuet
[Allegretto]

Gigue
[Allegro]

Gigue
from ENGLISH SUITE NO. 2 IN A MINOR

Johann Sebastian Bach
1685–1750

Menuet
from FRENCH SUITE NO. 3

Johann Sebastian Bach
1685–1750
BWV 814

[Allegretto]

[mp]

Trio

Menuet da capo

Prelude and Fugue No. 1 in C Major

from THE WELL-TEMPERED CLAVIER, BOOK I

Johann Sebastian Bach
1685-1750
BWV 846

Prelude
[Allegro]

Prelude and Fugue No. 1 in C Major
from THE WELL-TEMPERED CLAVIER, BOOK I

Johann Sebastian Bach
1685-1750
BWV 846

Prelude
[Allegro]

[mp]

Fugue (4 Voices)
[Andantino]

[mf]

[rit.]

Prelude and Fugue No. 2 in C Minor
from THE WELL-TEMPERED CLAVIER, BOOK I

Johann Sebastian Bach
1685-1750
BWV 871

Prelude
[Allegro]

[*f*]

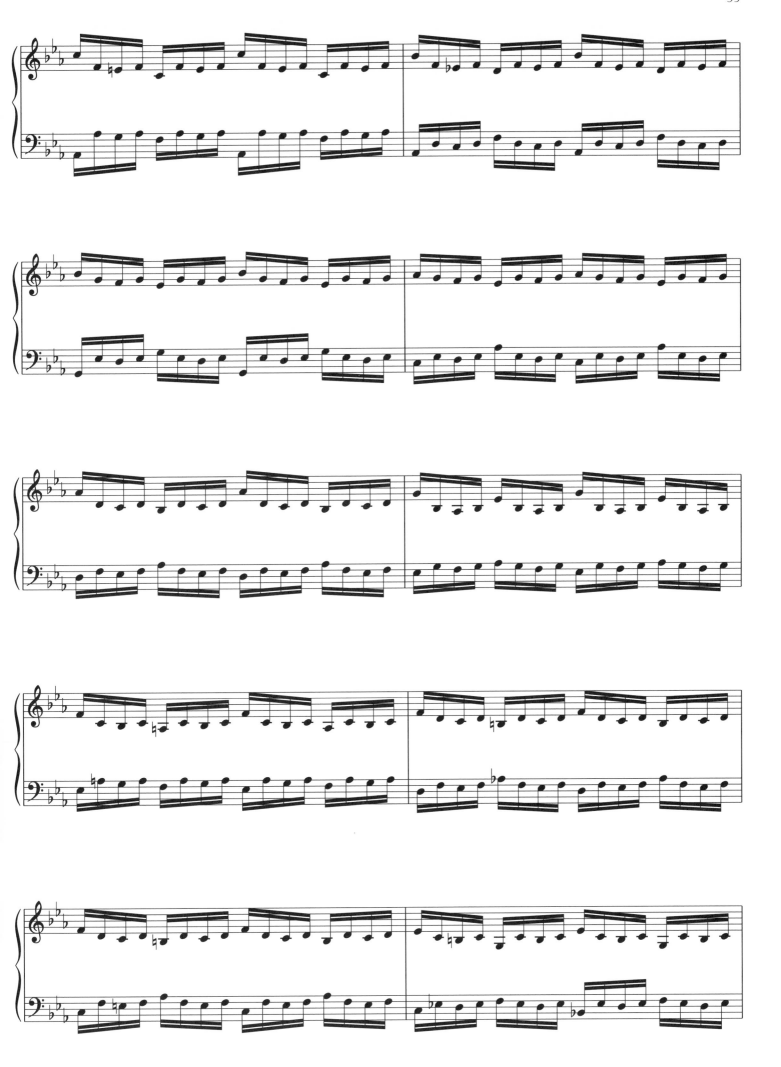

Presto

Fugue (3 Voices)
[Allegretto]

Prelude and Fugue No. 5 in D Major
from THE WELL-TEMPERED CLAVIER, BOOK I

Johann Sebastian Bach
1685-1750
BWV 850

Prelude
[Allegro]

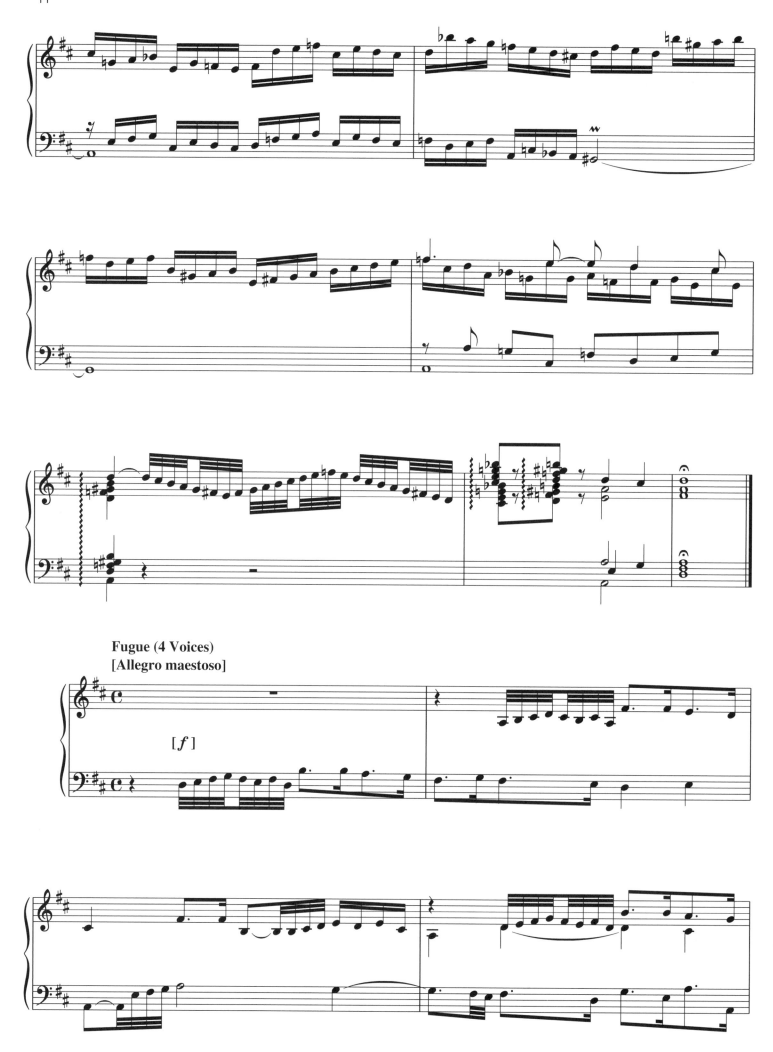

Fugue (4 Voices)
[Allegro maestoso]

[*f*]

Prelude and Fugue No. 11 in F Major
from THE WELL-TEMPERED CLAVIER, BOOK I

Johann Sebastian Bach
1685-1750
BWV 856

Prelude
[Allegro]

Fugue (3 Voices)
[Allegro]

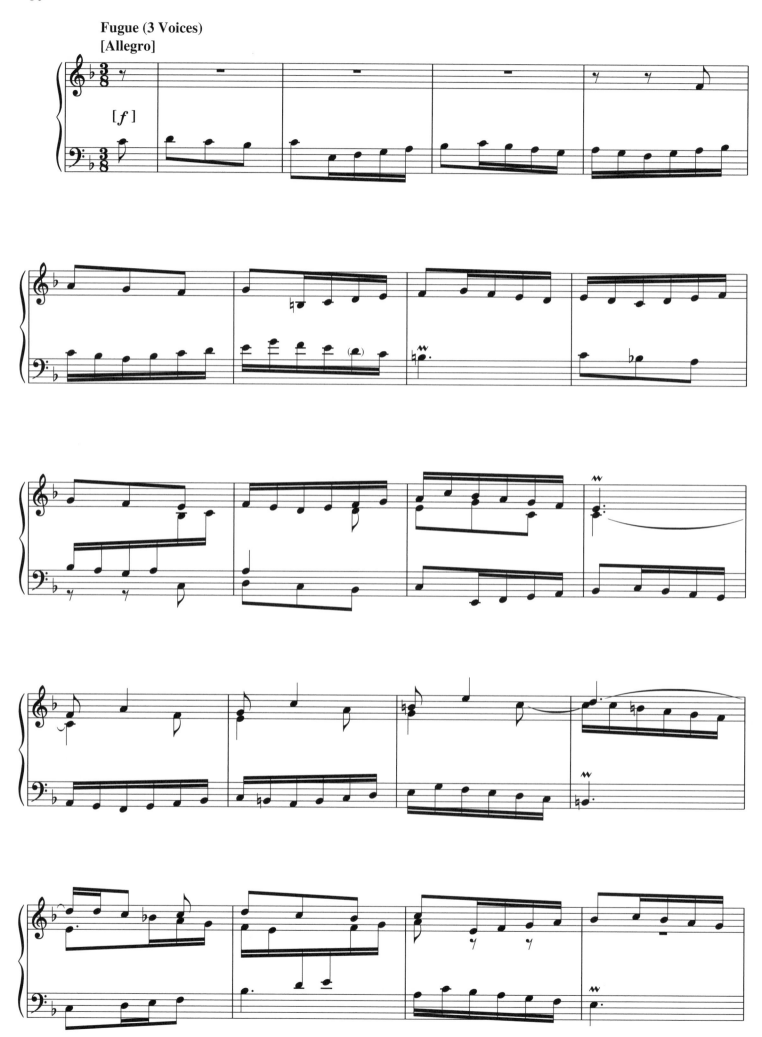

Prelude and Fugue No. 16 in G Minor

from THE WELL-TEMPERED CLAVIER, BOOK I

Johann Sebastian Bach
1685-1750
BWV 861

Prelude
[Andante]

[*mp*]

Fugue (4 Voices)
[Moderato]

[*mf*]

Prelude and Fugue No. 21 in B-flat Major

from THE WELL-TEMPERED CLAVIER, BOOK I

Johann Sebastian Bach
1685–1750
BWV 866

Prelude
[Allegro]

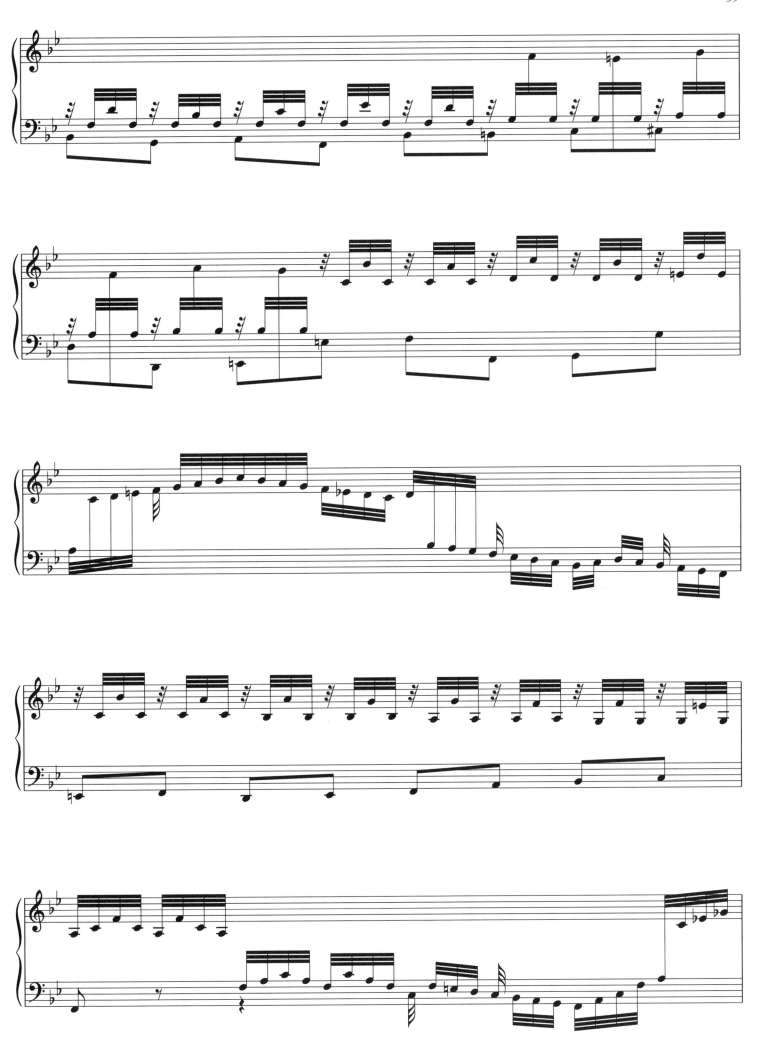

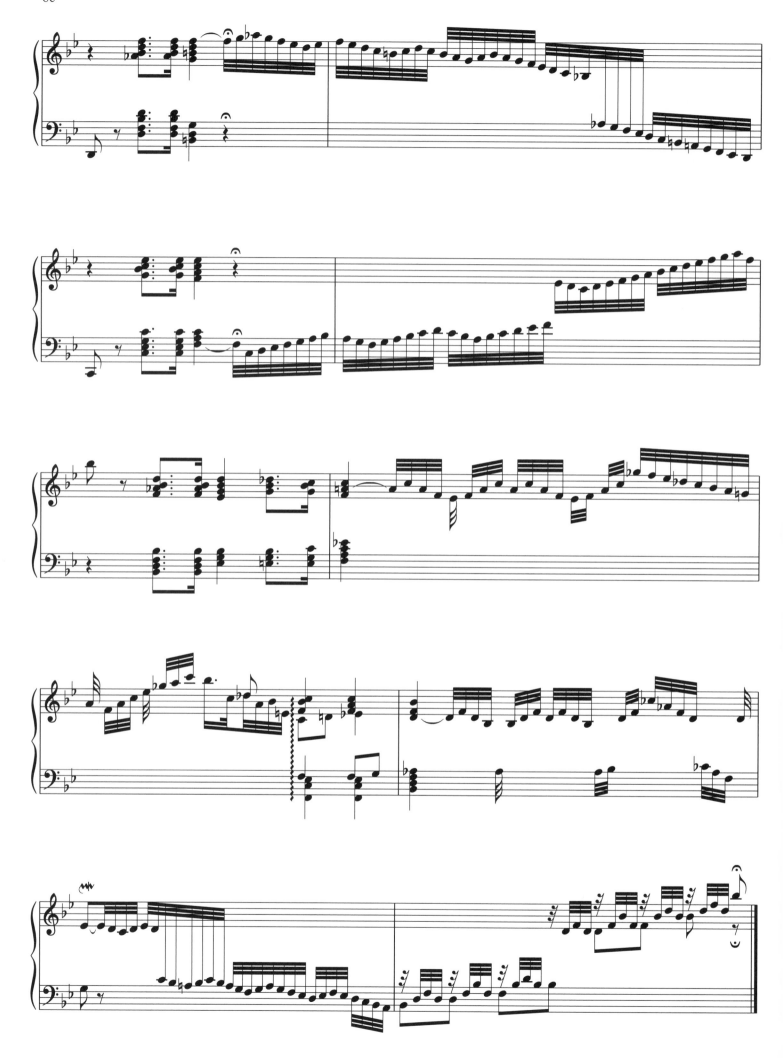

Fugue (3 Voices)
[Allegro]

The Alarm Clock
(Le réveil-matin)

François Couperin
1668–1733

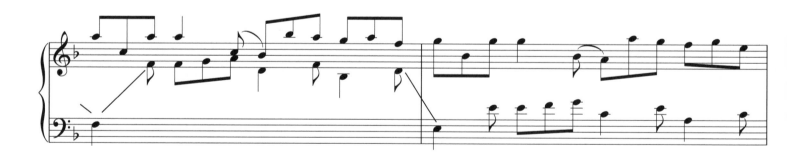

The Trophy
(Le trophée)

François Couperin
1668–1733

[Allegro Moderato]

[f]

Trifles
(Le petit-rien)

François Couperin
1668–1733

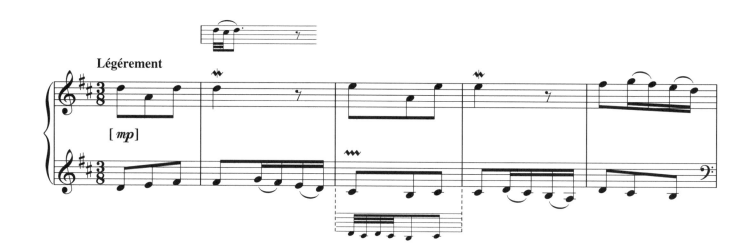

The Fifers
(Les fifres)

Jean-François Dandrieu
1682–1738

Dal Segno al Fine

The Flirt
(La coquette)

Jean-François Dandrieu
1682–1738

Allegro

Toccata and Fugue

Girolamo Frescobaldi
1583–1643

TOCCATA
[Allegro]

[f]

The toccata and fugue are separate works paired together for this publication.

FUGUE
[Moderato]

[*mf*]

Toccata

Johann Jacob Froberger
1616–1667

L'istesso tempo

Prelude and Fugue
from SUITE NO. 6 IN F-SHARP MINOR

George Frideric Handel
1685–1759

PRELUDE
Largo

FUGUE

Allegro

[*mf*]

Allemande, Sarabande and Gigue

Jean-Baptiste Lully
1632–1687

ALLEMANDE
Andante

[*mf*]

Play the grace notes on the beat.

SARABANDE

GIGUE
Molto allegro

Tender Song
(Air tendre)

Jean-Baptiste Lully
1632–1687

Courante

Jean-Baptiste Lully
1632–1687

*Play on the beat.

Suite No. 4 in A Minor

Henry Purcell
1659–1695
Z. 663

*Purcell's "shake,"

ALLEMANDE
[Moderato]

COURANTE
[Allegretto]

[mf]

*The grace note is played on the beat.

SARABANDE
[Andante]

Suite No. 6 in D Major

Henry Purcell
1659–1695
Z. 667

PRELUDE
[Allegro]

*played:

ALLEMANDE
[Moderato]

HORNPIPE

[Allegro]

Chaconne

Johann Pachelbel
1653–1706

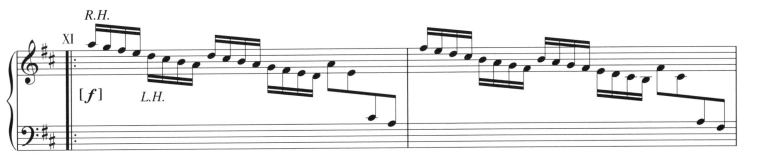

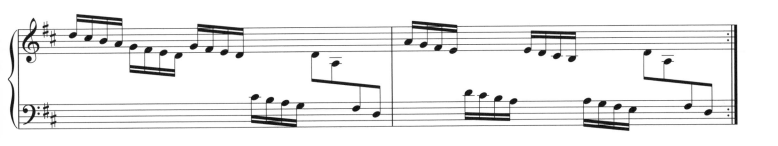

Fugue

Johann Pachelbel
1653–1706

The Egyptian Lady
(L' Égyptienne)
from NOUVELLES SUITES

Jean-Philippe Rameau
1683–1764

*The pincé, played: for short notes, for longer note values.

The Peasant Girl
(La villageoise)
from PIÈCES DE CLAVECIN

Jean-Philippe Rameau
1683–1764

[Moderato]

[mp]

*Rameau's pincé

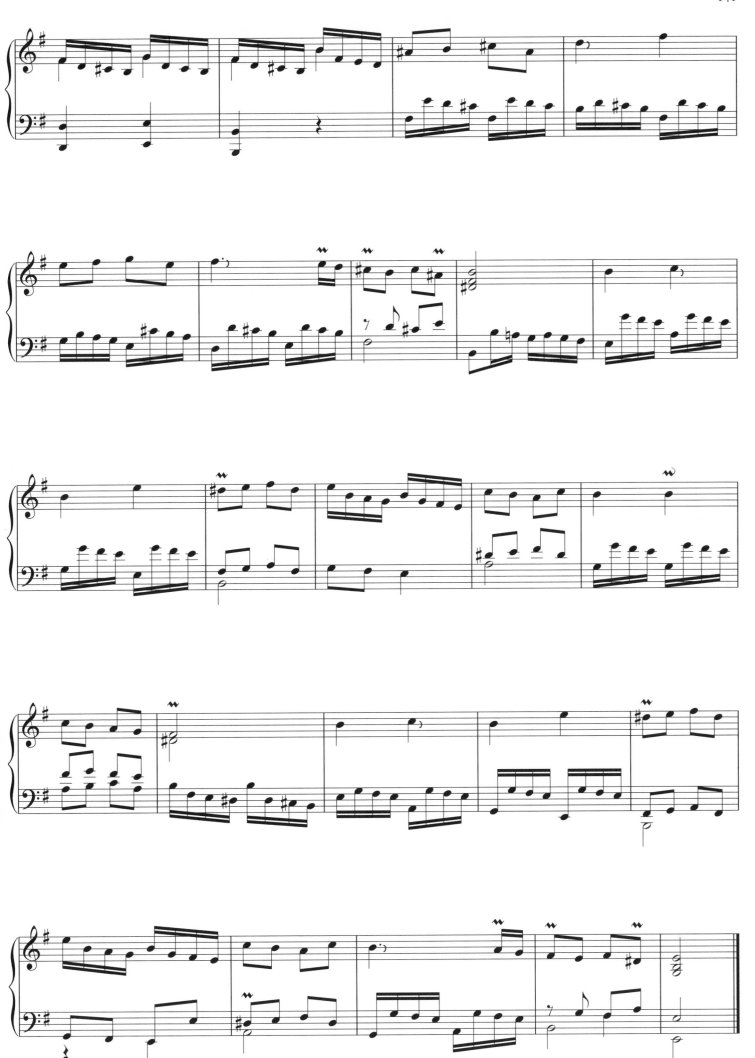

Bird Calls
(Les rappel des oiseaux)
from PIÈCES DE CLAVECIN

Jean-Phillipe Rameau
1683–1764

Allegro légèrement

The pincé, played:

Sonata in G Major

Domenico Scarlatti
1685–1757
L. 388 (K. 2, P. 58)

Sonata in E Major

Domenico Scarlatti
1685–1757
L. 23 (K. 380)

Sonata in E Minor

Domenico Scarlatti
1685–1757
L. 427 (K. 402, P. 496)

Andante

Sonata in E Major

Domenico Scarlatti
1685–1757
L. 470 (K. 403, P. 437)

Sonata in D Major

Domenico Scarlatti
1685–1757
L. 465 (K. 96)

mutandi i deti

Prelude
from CELLO SUITE NO. 1 IN G MAJOR

Johann Sebastian Bach
1685-1750
BWV 1007
originally for solo violoncello

Bourée I
from CELLO SUITE NO. 3 IN C MAJOR

Johann Sebastian Bach
1685-1750
BWV 1009
originally for solo violoncello

Air on the G String

from ORCHESTRAL SUITE NO. 3 IN D MAJOR

Johann Sebastian Bach
1685–1750
BWV 1068
originally for orchestra

Arioso
from KEYBOARD CONCERTO NO. 5 IN F MINOR

Johann Sebastian Bach
1685-1750
BWV 1056
originally for keyboard, strings and continuo

* This material was also adapted by Bach for his Cantata No. 156.

Jesu, Joy of Man's Desiring

(Jesus, bleibet meine Freude)

from Cantata No. 147, HERZ UND MUND UND TAT UND LEBEN

Johann Sebastian Bach
1685–1750
BWV 147
originally for choir and orchestra

Siciliano
from SONATA NO. 2 FOR FLUTE AND HARPSICHORD

Johann Sebastian Bach
1685-1750
BWV 1031

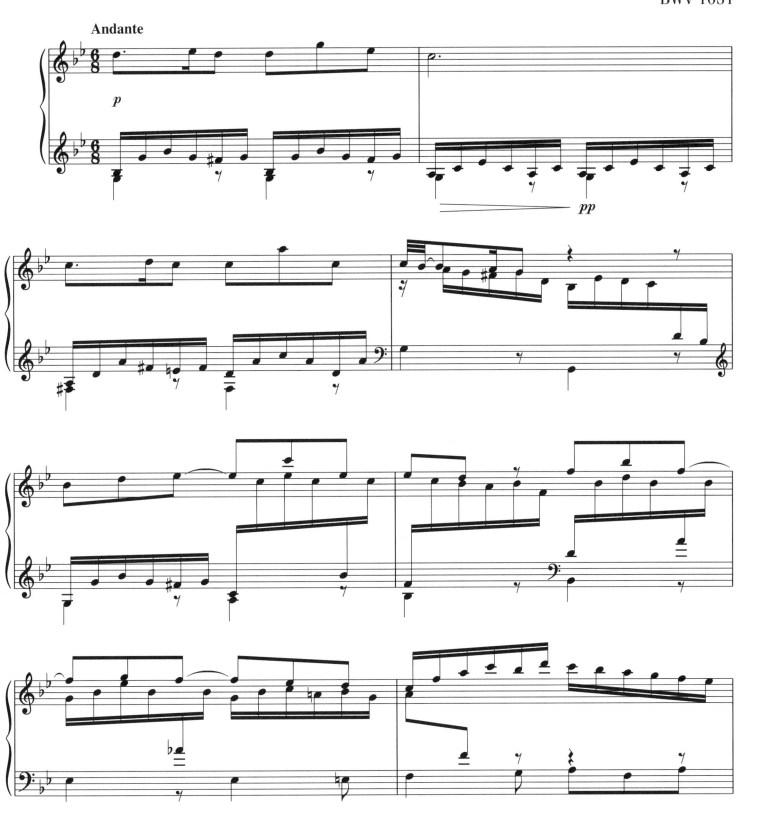

Sleepers, awake
from Cantata No. 140, WACHET AUF, RUFT UNS DIE STIMME

Johann Sebastian Bach
1685-1750
BWV 140
originally for tenor, strings and continuo

[poco rit.]

Allegro
from WATER MUSIC

George Frideric Handel
1685–1759
originally for orchestra

Air
from WATER MUSIC

George Frideric Handel
1685–1759
originally for orchestra

Andante con moto

Allegro Maestoso
from WATER MUSIC

GEORGE FRIDERIC HANDEL
1685–1759
originally for orchestra

Allegro maestoso

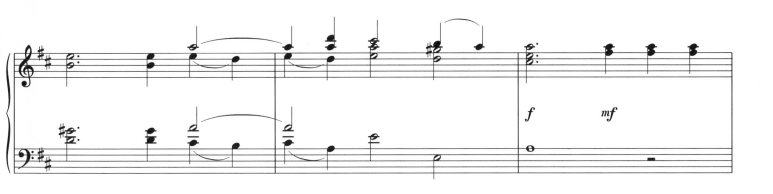

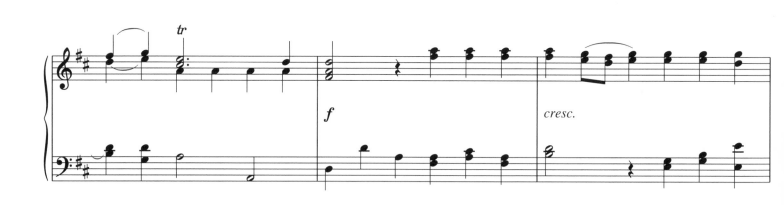

Hallelujah
from the oratorio MESSIAH

George Frideric Handel
1685–1759
originally for chorus and orchestra

Allegro moderato

Largo
(Ombra mai fù)
from the opera SERSE
(Xerxes)

George Frideric Handel
1685–1759
originally for alto voice and orchestra

Pastoral Symphony
from the oratorio MESSIAH

George Frideric Handel
1685-1759
originally for orchestra

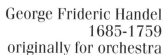

Rondeau
from the theatre music for ABDELAZER

Henry Purcell
1659-1695
originally for orchestra

* Main theme used by Benjamin Britten in his YOUNG PERSON'S GUIDE TO THE ORCHESTRA

Canon in D Major

Johann Pachelbel
1653-1706
originally for 3 violins and continuo

Adagio

Spring

from THE FOUR SEASONS
First Movement

Antonio Vivaldi
1678-1741
originally for violin & string orchestra

Autumn
from THE FOUR SEASONS
First Movement

Antonio Vivaldi
1678-1741
originally for violin and orchestra

Autumn
from THE FOUR SEASONS
Third Movement

Antonio Vivaldi
1678-1741
originally for violin & string orchestra

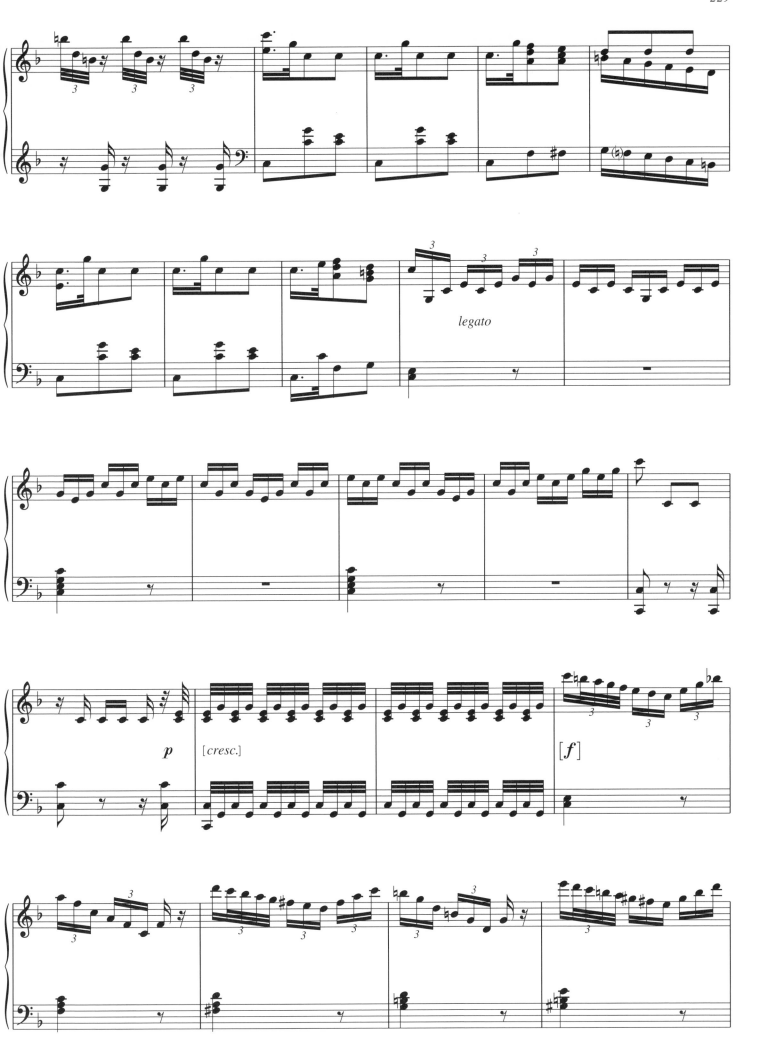

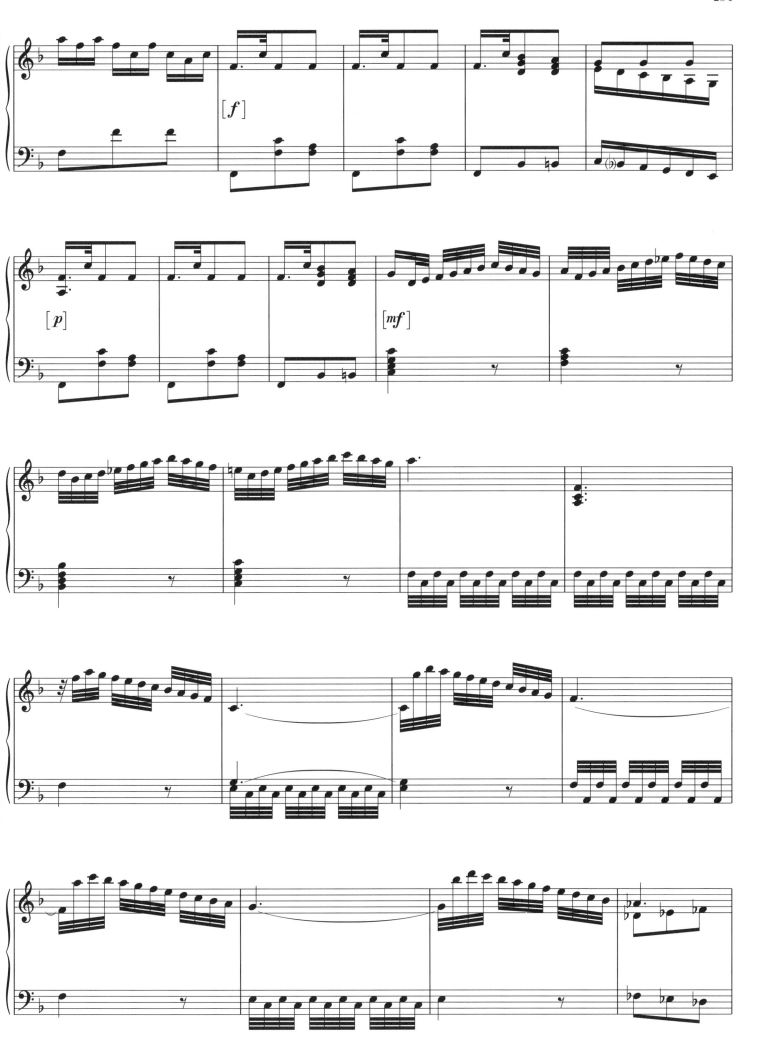